KALEIDO

Kandace Siobhan Walker's double pamphlet is a dextrous, inventive take on the tarot's Major Arcana. Mirrored in its entirety, *Kaleido* explores the archetypes in both upright and reversed positions—attesting to Walker's superb formal skill and compelling line in existential enquiry. Summoning spirit guides, girlhood ennui, quetiapine dreams and Minnie Riperton, this speaker seeks certainty in biblical gardens, noisy bars and fast Cadillacs, in South East London, Sapelo Island and the Brecon Beacons. *Kaleido* is an enthralling, unforgettable debut.

'*Kaleido* returns us to the roaring, bright intersections of subjecthood and reality, to love, its totems, collisions and puncture-wounds. These are poems of genuine, casual modernism, deft musicality, intelligence and attentiveness; Siobhan Walker's voice is extraordinary. This is a vanguard debut that has found its new language, and it is wonderful.'
Jack Underwood

'*Kaleido* is a sharp and palindromic examination of our contemporary moment—in it, medicine and occultism come together to make tourmaline the lives of those denied agency under capitalism. Across these poems the world is destroyed and reborn, obsolescence and pessimism are challenged, and innocuous items become totemic refrains as Walker draws luminance from the quotidian, depicting the beautiful and horrific intensities of trying to live now. Exploring the possibility of symbiosis between the human and the non-human, Walker collaborates with vibrant language to create something witty, rich, complex. This is politically incisive and lyrically exciting poetry.'
Susannah Dickey

'A master of wordplay and storytelling, in *Kaleido*, Walker flexes her poetry muscles offering powerful imagery and ideas that will return to you days after putting down this book. A wonderful collection of carefully-crafted language spells masquerading as poems.'

Hanan Issa

Kandace Siobhan Walker is a writer and artist of Jamaican, Canadian, Saltwater Geechee and Welsh heritage. She is an editor at *bath magg*. She was awarded a Wales Venice 10 Commission by Artes Mundi in 2022. She received an Eric Gregory Award and won The White Review Poet's Prize in 2021. She won the Guardian 4th Estate Short Story Prize in 2019 for her story 'Deep Heart'. Her work is published in *Ludd Gang*, *Bad Lilies* and *Magma*, among others. She is represented by Abi Fellows at The Good Literary Agency.

KALEIDO

Kaleido

Published by Bad Betty Press in 2022
www.badbettypress.com

All rights reserved

Kandace Siobhan Walker has asserted her right to be identified as the author of this work in accordance with Section 77 of the Copyright, Designs and Patents Act of 1988.

Cover illustration by Kandace Siobhan Walker

Printed and bound in the United Kingdom

A CIP record of this book is available from the British Library.

ISBN: 978-1-913268-33-6

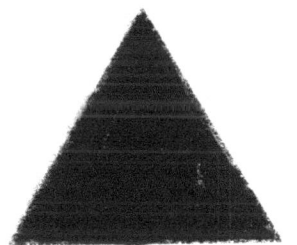

Contents

0 The Airhead	9
1 The Science	10
2 The Hag	11
3 The Dream	12
4 Reality	14
5 The Sisters	15
6 The Lovers	16
7 The Cadillac	17
8 The Heart	18
9 The Hermit	19
10 The World	20
11 The Sea	21
12 The Drowned	22
13 Birth	23
14 The Art	24
15 The Snake	25
16 The Academy	27
17 The Star	28
18 The Moon	30
19 The Sun	31
20 The Heavens	33
21 The Earth	34

o The Airhead

Rain, always a surprise.
Girlhood, an underpass

graffitied with angel-winged tags,
lovehearts like witnesses, woz here:

assertions of life as contemporary cuneiform.
It was clear the sky had some art.

I walked safely under the trees' shadow and
light, as it gave away secrets.

For gaze I blew pink bubblegum,
for knowledge I wept and made fists.

As complete and biblical as a garden,
I was young and right. I was freer than ribbon,

I skipped across wonder.
When the water surpassed the minutes,

I held another's hand,
was led out of that darkness

knowing what I did not yet know.
Soaked my homework through the bookbag,

dirtied my light-up trainers.

1 The Science

Relativity sparkling in my ears like diamonds,
I fell for the kings

of violence and fiction.
The original war against the sky

crows
no name, no generation except

adoration. Why
is the spirit of the light

as dictatorial as a mosquito
wing in tree sap,

the past
disguising coal as jewellery?

Images are all too willing
to wage, with loss as after-

thought, death.
An encounter—

during which
I felt observable

in front of an unscientific being,
the once was all it took—

with god.

2 The Hag

The sea is such an erotic blue
when breathing feels psychotic.

Heaven-dark nights charm
the genie out of a bottle of red:

footwork for the
low-waged and suicidal.

Sleeping at midday
feels like wind on my cheeks.

Dirty laundry voodoo,
chewing tablets like

tobacco and age
harmonising in a copper bowl:

office work for the conjureperson
kills the snake in my garden.

Delaying texts and emails
until my depression starts getting out of bed,

showering at last, doing her makeup,
posting a selfie.

Here's the ocean at the door.

3 The Dream

is water's ancestral spirit playing on white clapboard.
Earth beneath the oak tree that never dries.

Wayne Wonder in the walkman skipping as you jump the stones
across the stream to a pine meadow where your aunt sings

god and mercy from the bandstand.
Water balloons at the garden tap recalling some future

water fight in the green leaf air after a birthday.
We're twenty-three, we're eight, we're getting kinda faithful,

yeah, I keep a broken acrylic nail in the pocket of my jeans
because we're not getting any wiser, just more beautiful.

O, to be hotboxing deep love and early traumas
in that blue summer light, the lesser auroras

of Cancer season dawns. Garden shed, confessional.
The priest is the person who asks, Who wants the water?

People in movies know why you lose what you lose,
but we just lose. Not dreamers of the dream, just stewards.

The ground, cool and soft with the memory of the oak's
shadow we paid the tree surgeon to fell after a summer storm.

Running home with the rain and tonda pinned to your soles.
The obsolete wonder of a shimmering compact disc

lost downstream before you can catch up to the music.

4 Reality

Always a moment as I wake when, between two selves, I know
everything. Was I prepared to take action in service of this

knowledge? When I was immaterial and borderless and asking who
I wanted to love? A voice in space that wasn't not god but everywhere:

great barrier reefs of wages and sex and everyday struggle.
Spirits fly around the bedroom. I have too many feelings

to keep holding onto me. I'm so hungover, something gorgeous is fading:
that wide certainty. What was there to understand? Heaventheinvisibleworld,

return—waking with a kaleidoscopic awareness,
deep mongrel blue like aquarium tunnels, bedroom haunted by a

hierarchy of angels and ancestors swimming past like festival lanterns.

5 The Sisters

Birth of the swan: sleepy at the mountain's feet,
wake in her hair on quetiapine, wake red,

like a porpoise caught in the propellers.
The rules of the road are naught for casualties.

We all kneel for the face of a princess, why do you think
brothers wear amulets at the waist all their lives?

Crystals at the end of the string swing in a circle
for the daughter's question. The giants chew slow,

swallow a servant and vomit a poet. A strength
of our species is its ability to build churches

out of whatever washes up on the beach. In another millennium,
we'll hear orchestras play our violations to a live audience.

See—even when I'm dead, someone is willing
to unfold the white cloth shrouding my power

to balm their own grief.

6 The Lovers

It is the weekend, which means we must go
to where our friends are living now and drink pinot grigio.

We have abstract conversations about the future,
also adolescence, that which no longer holds us

and what holds us now—each other, with a spare set of keys.
We, running low on wine, make the trip to the corner shop,

talking about art and the people we date
and whatever the internet is arguing about today.

Even when the last train has passed and it is time for hugs and taxis,
we look out at the city—without sound, but not without listening.

We aren't unlike a rare alignment of planets—which means
we are lucky in the way that everyone needs to be lucky,

when it is the weekend, and whether or not we have slept,
seen the sun in days, means nothing, because now

we are leaving for the bus to go see our friends.

7 The Cadillac

Faster! In the wind,
pink headscarf

hung from the rearview,
real dice, seafoam. Interior,

valley. In the backseat,
a fork. In the river,

like a finish line ribbon,
like wind in the desert.

If you touch me I will break.
Abstinence as a melting ice cap,

lack of boundaries as a nightcap
against helpline hold music.

Exhaust fumes smell like self-reflection
enough to forgive myself.

I can't wake up from this dream
where I get out of the car

and keep running.

8 The Heart

Even peacocks get lonely.
Deep space is seen only by a telescope

in the desert. Years cosplaying an extrovert,
to realise there is closeness

and then there is proximity.
Yearning will be my magnum opus,

I fear. All the evenings I lived will haunt me
as a pink headscarf tied to the roof beam and the window

and my neck.
A flying sadness.

The world as puzzling as diamonds
cut into headlights,

a door handle that will not turn.
Waves swallowing friends and lovers like roman candles,

unaware I wasn't a system of caves.

9 The Hermit

Radio silence from my spirit guides.
My mothers leave flowers in my room

while I sleep, dreaming of burial at sea, painted
-shut windows, fuzzy blue ceiling damp,

a canoe with a glass skirt, a burning arrow.
I go around the house bleeding radiators,

the crated dog barks all night. In reality,
not wisdom, I have been lying

next to a pile of clean washing
for weeks. I wake up holding rosemary,

violas, fennel and doves. The water has
leeched all the green from the rotting stalks,

drained the pink from the gerbera's face, and
stained the vase with a heart and veins but

just now, entering the charts, a song about death.

10 The World

When I find it, I will say the words, and trap it,
like cave drawings animated by flame.

And there is a word, too, for light in the trees
and I let this bring me peace.

I let this radicalise me.
Is what erodes me

the spirit's inescapability,
this cursed amphora of poetry?

Whip of the wind when it wants you,
lychee fruit of daddies,

pink of wise women,
black over the beacons,

friend's dream of me,
dream of a friend,

blue sky feeling,
the four-leaf clover of a parakeet?

It's *all* luck and waiting.

ii The Sea

It rains to bring us together,
under the red imperial pavilion,

like bobbin lace.
The other couples are silent

in their whiteness and coupleness
and diplomatic love.

In the park you wear my denim jacket,
half a daydream.

Kids learn early
the truth about sunshine.

Space is a rearview mirror
but under skylights and mud roofs,

I wish to be different
while you sleep in a light that's already past.

Astronauts are wiser than we are.
From an airplane over the Atlantic,

it's easy to recognise honesty—
like dolphins tripping over dominoes.

I concede—I don't know what this feeling is.

12 The Drowned

All these images of death
are still death.

Three grey dots, millions
of black squares.

Does rope mourn
if I hang? Does water care if I drown?

The dhow ridge
of a bent back

as the mode of
arrival.

Water
is history.

I am already someone's ancestor.

13 Birth

Brother Blue's caterpillar had never heard of god.
He believed in dying 'til he tried it on.

His ugliness learned to admire itself.
The spirit and the physical: nothing is lost.

Or, butterfly. Or, being. Or, wowee, I'm beautiful! Or,
the ground wedded to the sky. Death in the night means

a birth in the morning. It is only the world turning on her axis.
Like the caterpillar sleepwalking in crystal, shrouded eyes

ignoring the white horse and the black standard,
the setting sun. Look away and you'll see:

dayclean. Night cleared away. Or, chrysalis.
Or, a homegoing. Or, maybe, waking somewhere else,

the first rays of light streaking across the sky.

14 The Art

Affirmations, bestie. Say it with me:
I will be transparent

about my monastic ambitions,
hold out against the urge to rain hellfire.

I will slackline across the suburban rooftops
of my teenage enemies, I will fall, I will ring the doorbell,

I will be welcomed, I will eat breakfast
with the family, sleep on their sofa for several months,

stop projecting hostility, learn
to sit with how I feel.

I will share my Halloween candy, I will
hoard nothing.

I will haunt my hometown like a moon
on a summer evening. I will take

kindness wherever it is offered and I will not question
whether or not I deserve it.

I will be thankful
for the house I was raised in, and remember

I don't live there anymore.

15 The Snake

An event in the sky.
Everything is shrouded.

The city is a siesta.
I wander hours

without conversation,
like a hungry person

among lotus-eaters.
I wave away a street vendor

selling eclipse viewers.
It is how I have always lived.

By twilight, by static,
by that kind of prayer

that leads down a well.
Creator-gods are given too much

praise, or not enough
depending on the hemisphere.

With evening,
the hieroglyphic noise

rides in, but for a few sympathetic minutes,
everyone walks around as if stoned,

blinking like babies.

16 The Academy

Capitalism is working—
we had too many rainforests,

we needed fewer exotic animals.
We needed more austerities

like food deserts and mandatory minimums,
retirement ages vanishing behind the Earth's curvature.

What we need are fewer ecosystems!
Hunter-gatherers never built a sky pool.

Revolutions are unproductive, that's why
I'm working only on myself now,

by which I mean I'm getting sexier.
Suffering? I don't know her.

By which I mean, I don't want to be orphaned by
a century inside the heart of an iceberg,

waking up to the war.

17 The Star

I search and search the wet streets,
asking strangers

of what we have lost. I find myself in
reflections of taillights like an oil painting.

Now people are television.
Even winter is a snake-charmer,

the media says. Wealth is irrelevant,
says the state.

Class war is easy,
its instructions are clear

and impossible.
Even grief is an approximation now.

The wind blurs my fingers,
multiplying

the eyes of my lovers.
Without my friends,

I am a tunnel of ghosts.
Cool-white pinpricks begin

to defy the dark, a dream
of spring maturing like newspaper, and

the sound of voices.

18 The Moon

I love strangers, noisy bars, busy streets,
but my brain goes   whenever

someone addresses me. I want to cry:
let me in! Person-first or label-first,

either's cool with me, I death-drive on confusion.
And I miss my green football pitches

on a big flatscreen so, men in synthetic
perforated jerseys. Cheap tobacco,

blue smell of pool cue chalk, cool glass.
Every experience is an atomised list.

I miss the social cues I always missed.
Walking back to a new friend's flat,

talking the West, talking eyeshadow.
Hut-hut. Sound of happiness. Taste of rain.

I never learned the rules of any game.

19 The Sun

We are maybe the worst people alive,
attractive and self-expectant.

Nobody votes for us except each other.
I admire the party of my friendships,

eggshell and elastic like anthers and
springtime at the bar.

A man asks who I know here.
Everything is so easy

because we are young.
Living is its own authority.

We sing *will somebody wear me to the fair*,
and *baby love, my—* and *bad girls*.

On the bus, we sing *mi haffi work,
work, work, work, work, work*.

Next week, we will
put in our earphones and frown but

today the colours of the sky,
from a condemned car park

or a strangers' balcony,
catch us like a free bar.

We don't care if we wake up
on someone's hardwood floor

because we fear we will
never grow old, never grow,

so tomorrow means tonight.

20 The Heavens

The green fields are like intimacy
disturbing the leaves and my lips.

I arrive again at the end
of an ordinary life.

Weary in her kabaslot,
my ancestor refuses

to be sent down another time.
She is done. But I am

reincarnated as a blindfolded river,
a starwhale, a nothing-bagel.

Three pretty clouds asking to be judged,
then a hollow horse. Then my own daughter,

forgetting everything each time.
The blue cities are like a kiss

dying and suffering in me.
I always hear the call, and

answer.

21 The Earth

We are such pretty Earthlings, we have the keys
to the kingdom jangling in the ignition.

Disorder will judge me, but I want television
after the revolution. I want my haint blue cadillac

to run off water and light and air. Forty acres of day-
dreaming and a water pump, a garden for the mule to plow.

Who stands while we kneel? Who is unfree when we live free?
Future geographies will recall how we asked

for everything. Unstick yourself from the seat,
unzip yourself, undone. I wish for the next -ocene

to be easy in all the ways living should be easy.
Living creatures are just angels with names,

realities are granted all the clemency of statehood
and all their sexy palaces. In a million years

we'll be dust. But we will have killed the saints
so deep, so good, heaven will be obsolete.

The world is a fiction. Overturn the cup!

21 The Earth

The world is a fiction. Overturn the cup
so deep, so good, heaven will be obsolete.

We'll be dust, but we will have killed the saints
and all their sexy palaces. In a million years,

realities are granted all the clemency of statehood,
living creatures are just angels with names.

To be easy in all the ways living should be easy,
unzip yourself, undone. I wish for the next -ocene,

for everything. Unstick yourself from the seat,
future geographies will recall how we asked

who kneels while we stand? Who is free when we live unfree?
Dreaming and a water pump, a garden for the mule to plow.

To run off water and light and air, forty acres of day.
After the revolution, I want my haint blue cadillac.

Disorder will judge me, but I want television.
To the kingdom jangling in the ignition:

we are such pretty Earthlings. We have the keys.

20 The Heavens

Answer.
I always hear the call of

dying and suffering. In me,
the blue cities are like a kiss,

forgetting everything each time.
Then a hollow horse, then a daughter.

Three pretty clouds asking to be judged,
a starwhale, a nothing-bagel

reincarnated as a blindfolded river.
She is done, but I am

to be sent down another time.
My ancestor refuses,

weary in her kabaslot
of an ordinary life.

I arrive again at the end,
disturbing the leaves and my lips.

The green fields are like intimacy.

19 The Sun

So tomorrow means tonight
never grows old, never grows.

Because we fear we will,
on someone's hardwood floor.

We don't care if we wake up,
catch us like a free bar

or a stranger's balcony.
From a condemned car park,

today the colours of the sky
put in our earphones and frown. But

next week, we will
work, work, work, work, work,

on the bus, we sing *mi haffi work*
and *baby love, my—* and *bad girls*,

we sing *will somebody wear me to the fair.*
Living is its own authority

because we are young.
Everything is so easy,

a man asks who I know here.
Springtime at the bar,

eggshell and elastic like anthers, and
I admire the party of my friendships.

Nobody votes for us except each other.
Attractive and self-expectant,

we may be the worst people alive.

18 The Moon

I never learned the rules of any game.
Hut-hut. Sound of happiness. Taste of rain.

Talking the West, talking eyeshadow.
Walking back to a new friend's flat,

I miss the social cues I always missed.
Every experience is an atomised list:

blue smell of pool cue chalk, cool glass,
perforated jerseys, cheap tobacco

on a big flatscreen, 20 men in synthetic.
And I miss my green, football pitches,

either's cool. With me, I death-drive on confusion.
Let me in. Person-first or label-first,

someone addresses me. I want to cry
but my brain goes   whenever

I love. Strangers, noisy. Bars, busy. Streets.

17 The Star

The sound of voices,
of spring maturing like newspaper

to defy the dark. A dream,
cool-white pinpricks. Begin.

I am a tunnel of ghosts
without my friends,

the eyes of lovers.
Multiplying the wind

blurs my fingers,
even grief. It's an approximation now,

and impossible.
Its instructions are clear.

Class war is easy,
says the state.

The media says wealth is irrelevant.
Even winter is a snake-charmer.

Now people are television,
reflections of taillights. Like an oil painting

of what we have lost, I find myself in asking strangers.

I search and search the wet streets.

16 The Academy

Waking up to the war,
a century inside the heart of an iceberg.

By which I mean, I don't want to be orphaned by
suffering. I don't know her,

by which I mean, I'm getting sexier.
I'm working only on myself now.

Revolutions are unproductive, that's why
hunter-gatherers never built a sky pool.

What we need are fewer ecosystems,
retirement ages vanishing behind the Earth's curvature

like food deserts and mandatory minimums.
We needed more austerities,

we needed fewer exotic animals.
We had too many rainforests.

Capitalism is working.

15 The Snake

Blinking like babies,
everyone walks around as if stoned.

Riding in, for a few sympathetic minutes,
the hieroglyphic noise

of evening.
Depending on the hemisphere:

praise, or not enough.
Creator-gods are given too much

that leads down a well.
By that kind of prayer,

by twilight, by static,
is how I have always lived—

selling eclipse viewers.
I wave away a street vendor

among lotus-eaters
like a hungry person

without conversation.
I wander hours,

the city is a siesta,
everything is shrouded.

An event in the sky.

14 The Art

I don't live there anymore.
For the house I was raised in and remember,

I will be thankful
whether or not I deserve it.

Kindness, wherever it is offered, I will not question.
On a summer evening, I will take,

I will haunt. My hometown, like a moon,
hoards nothing.

I will share my Halloween candy, I will
sit with how I feel,

stop projecting hostility. Learn
with the family. Sleep on their sofa. For several months.

I will be welcomed, I will eat breakfast
with my teenage enemies, I will fall, I will ring the doorbell,

I will slackline across the suburban rooftops,
hold out against the urge to rain hellfire.

About my monastic ambitions,
I will be transparent.

Affirmations, bestie. Say it with me.

13 Birth

The first rays of light streaking across the sky.
Or, a homegoing. Or, maybe, waking somewhere else.

Dayclean, night cleared away. Or, chrysalis,
the setting sun. Look away and you'll see—

ignoring the white horse and the black standard,
like the caterpillar sleepwalking in crystal—shrouded eyes.

A birth in the morning, it is only the world. Turning on her axis,
the ground wedded to the sky. Death in the night means

butterfly, or being, or wowee, I'm beautiful! Or,
the spirit and the physical: nothing is lost.

His ugliness learned to admire itself.
He believed in dying 'til he tried it on.

Brother Blue's caterpillar had never heard of god.

12 The Drowned

I am already someone's ancestor.
Is history

water?
Arrival

as the mode of
a bent back's

dhow ridge.
If I hang, does water care? If I drown,

does rope mourn?
Black squares,

three grey dots, millions
are still dead.

All these images of death.

ii The Sea

I concede—I don't know what this feeling is,
like dolphins tripping over dominoes.

It's easy to recognise honesty
from an airplane over the Atlantic.

Astronauts are wiser than we are,
while you sleep in a light that's already past.

I wish to be different
but under skylights and mud roofs,

space is a rearview mirror.
The truth about sunshine

kids learn early.
Half a daydream.

In the park you wear my denim jacket
and diplomatic love.

In their whiteness and coupleness,
the other couples are silent

like bobbin lace.
Under the red imperial pavilion,

it rains to bring us together.

10 The World

It's all luck and waiting:
the four-leaf clover of a parakeet,

blue sky feeling,
friend's dream of me,

dream of a friend,
black over the beacons.

Pink of wise women,
lychee fruit of daddies,

whip of the wind when it wants you,
this cursed amphora of poetry.

The spirit's inescapability
is what erodes me.

I let this radicalise me,
and I let this bring me peace.

And there is a word, too, for light in the trees,
like cave drawings animated by flame.

When I find it, I will say the words, and trap it.

9 The Hermit

Just now, entering the charts, a song about death
stained the vase with a heart and veins but

drained the pink from the gerbera's face. And
leeched all the green from the rotting stalks.

Violas, fennel and doves. The water.
For weeks I wake up holding rosemary

next to a pile of clean washing,
not wisdom. I have been lying.

The crated dog barks all night. As reality,
I go around the house bleeding radiators.

A canoe with a glass skirt, a burning arrow,
shut windows, fuzzy blue ceiling damp

while I sleep. Dreaming of burial at sea, painted.
My mothers leave flowers in my room.

Radio silence from my spirit guides.

8 The Heart

Unaware I wasn't a system of caves,
waves swallowing friends and lovers like Roman candles,

a door handle that will always turn,
cut into headlights,

the world was as puzzling as diamonds.
A flying sadness,

and my neck
as a pink headscarf tied to the roof beam and the window.

I fear all the evenings I lived will haunt me.
Yearning will be my magnum opus.

And then there is proximity.
To realise there is closeness

in the desert years. Cosplaying an extrovert
is deep space. Seen only by a telescope,

even peacocks get lonely.

7 The Cadillac

Keep running.
When I get out of the car,

I can't wake up from the dream
enough to forgive myself.

Exhaust fumes smell like self-reflection
against helpline hold music.

Lack of boundaries as a nightcap,
abstinence as a melting ice cap.

I will break. If you touch me
like wind in the desert,

like a finish line ribbon,
fork in the river.

Valley in the backseat,
seafoam interior, real dice

hung from the rearview.
Pink headscarf

in the wind. Faster!

6 The Lovers

We are leaving for the bus to go see our friends.
Seen in the sun, days mean nothing, because now,

when it is the weekend, whether or not we have slept,
we are lucky in the way that everyone needs to be lucky.

We aren't unlike a rare alignment of planets, which means
we look out at the city. Without sound, but not without listening,

even when the last train has passed and it is time for hugs and taxis
and whatever the internet is arguing about today.

Talking about art and the people we date,
we, running low on wine, make the trip to the corner shop.

And what holds us now? Each other, with a spare set of keys.
Also adolescence, that which no longer holds us.

We have abstract conversations about the future
where our friends are living now and drink pinot grigio.

It is the weekend, which means we must go.

5 The Sisters

to balm their own grief,
unfold the white cloth shrouding my power.

See—even when I'm dead, someone is willing.
We'll hear orchestras play our violations to a live audience,

out of whatever washes up on the beach in another millennium
of our species. Is its ability to build churches,

swallow a servant and vomit a poet, a strength?
For the daughter's question, the giants chew slow.

Crystals at the end of the string swing in a circle,
brothers wear amulets at the waist all their lives.

We all kneel for the face of a princess. Why do you think
the rules of the road are naught? For casualties,

like a porpoise caught in the propellers,
wake in her hair. On quetiapine, wake red.

Birth of the swan: sleepy at the mountain's feet.

4 Reality

Hierarchy of angels and ancestors swimming past like festival lanterns.
Deep mongrel blue like aquarium tunnels, bedroom haunted by a

return; waking; a kaleidoscopic awareness.
This wide certainty. What is there to understand? Heaventheinvisible. World,

keep holding onto me, I'm so hungover. Something gorgeous is fading.
Spirits, fly around the bedroom, I have too many feelings—

great barrier reefs of wages and sex and everyday struggle.
I wanted to love a voice in space that wasn't not god but everywhere.

Knowledge, when I was immaterial and borderless and asking who
everything was. I prepared to take action in service of this

always, a moment as I wake when, between two selves, I know.

3 The Dream

lost downstream before you can catch up to the music.
The obsolete wonder of a shimmering compact disc

running home with the rain and tonda pinned to your soles.
Shadow, we paid the tree surgeon to fell a summer storm.

The ground, cool and soft with the memory of the oaks.
We just lose. Not dreamers of the dream, just stewards,

people in movies. Know why you lose what you lose:
the priest is the person who asks, who wants the water

of Cancer season dawns, garden shed confessional
in that blue summer light? The lesser auroras,

o, to be hotboxing deep love and early traumas.
We're not getting any wiser, just more beautiful.

Yeah, I keep a broken acrylic nail in the pocket of my jeans,
we're getting kinda faithful. We're twenty-three, we're eight:

Water fight in the green leaf air after a birthday.
Water balloons at the garden tap recalling some future

god and mercy from the bandstand.
Across the stream to a pine meadow where your aunt sings

Wayne Wonder. The walkman jumping as you skip the stones.
Earth beneath the oak tree that never dries

is water's ancestral spirit playing on white clapboard.

2 The Hag

Here's the ocean at the door,
posting a selfie,

showering at last, doing her makeup
until my depression starts getting out of bed.

Delaying texts and emails
kills the snake in my garden.

Office work for the conjureperson
harmonising in a copper bowl.

Tobacco and age,
chewing tablets like

dirty laundry voodoo.
Feels like wind on my cheeks.

Sleeping at midday,
low-waged and suicidal:

rootwork for the
genie out of a bottle of red.

Heaven-dark nights charm
when breathing feels psychotic.

The sea is such an erotic blue.

1 The Science

With god
the once was all it took—

in front of an unscientific being,
I felt observable.

During which,
an encounter—

thought, death,
to wage. With loss as after-

images. Are we all too willing,
disguising coal as jewellery?

The past,
a wing in tree sap,

as dictatorial as a mosquito.
Is the spirit of the light

adoration? Why
no name, no generation except

crows?
The original war against the sky

of violence and fiction.

o The Airhead

Dirtied my light-up trainers,
soaked my homework through the bookbag,

knowing what I did not yet know,
and was led out of that darkness.

I held another's hand
when the water surpassed the minutes.

I skipped across wonder,
I was freer than ribbon. I was young and right,

as complete and biblical as a garden.
For knowledge I wept and made fists,

for gaze I blew pink bubblegum.
Light, as it gave away secrets

and the trees' shadow, I walked safely under.
It was clear the sky had some art.

Assertions of life as contemporary cuneiform:
lovehearts like witnesses, woz here

graffitied with angel-winged tags,
girlhood. An underpass.

Rain, always a surprise.

Contents

0 The Airhead	60
1 The Science	59
2 The Hag	58
3 The Dream	56
4 Reality	55
5 The Sisters	54
6 The Lovers	53
7 The Cadillac	52
8 The Heart	51
9 The Hermit	50
10 The World	49
11 The Sea	48
12 The Drowned	47
13 Birth	46
14 The Art	45
15 The Snake	43
16 The Academy	42
17 The Star	40
18 The Moon	39
19 The Sun	37
20 The Heavens	36
21 The Earth	35

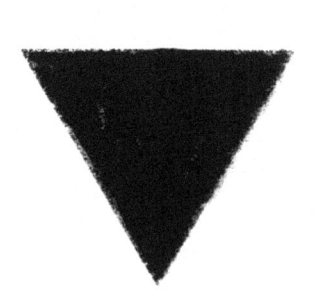

Kaleido

Published by Bad Betty Press in 2022
www.badbettypress.com

All rights reserved

Kandace Siobhan Walker has asserted her right to be identified as the author of this work in accordance with Section 77 of the Copyright, Designs and Patents Act of 1988.

Cover illustration by Kandace Siobhan Walker

Printed and bound in the United Kingdom

A CIP record of this book is available from the British Library.

ISBN: 978-1-913268-33-6

Supported using public funding by
ARTS COUNCIL ENGLAND
LOTTERY FUNDED

KALEIDO

BAD BETTY PRESS

Notes

Earlier versions of '21 The Earth' and '16 The Academy' appeared in *Poetry Wales*.

The line 'the first rays of light streaking across the sky' in '13 Birth' is borrowed, with love, from *God, Dr. Buzzard and the Bolito Man* by Cornelia Walker Bailey.

KALEIDO

Acknowledgements

Thank you to my publishers, Amy and Jake of Bad Betty Press, for welcoming Kaleido into the world. To my agent Abi and everyone at The Good Literary Agency.

To the people I love, for their kindness and their weirdness and their company. Alex, Daisy, Dill, Durre, Eliza, Ellie, Farrah, Franca, Georgia, Khemi, Naomi, Sherrie, Steph: you're all absolute babes. Especially to Hanan, Jack and Susie, thanks for saying nice things about these poems and also for being yourselves. And I'm thankful for all of the other writers and artists that I have been privileged to work with, and whose approaches to creative practice have altered and shifted the way I think and write and live.

To my far-flung family: thank you. To those who have passed, my aunt Andrea and my uncle Menelik and my grandmother Cornelia, for gifts that reach too deep to honour with language. Thank you especially to my little sister Josie, and to my parents: Marva, Stephen and Stanley for making me alive, and for everything else since.

Thank you to the tarot, for the questions it asks. And also apologies to the cards, for always trying to rig the answers. And thank you, whoever you are, for reading this book. May you overturn many cups, may you find the keys.

Milton Keynes UK
Ingram Content Group UK Ltd.
UKHW010156050324
438811UK00005B/104